To the human beings who are
joyfully creating the New Earth,
in themselves and in their
everyday lives.

Isn't it kind of funny that...

By
Jerry Schaefer

Illustrated by
Gabriel Berrón

expandjoy.com

SHIRES ● PRESS

4869 Main Street
P.O. Box 2200
Manchester Center, VT 05255
www.northshire.com

ISBN: 978-1-60571-594-0

Illustrated by Gabriel Berrón www.imagencontacto.com

Layout/production by Anne Pace pace@vermontel.net

Printed in the United States
November 2021

Isn't it kind of funny that...

we have
everything
we need
for
everyone
on earth
to have
everything
they could
possibly
need to be
healthy
and happy
and yet...
we aren't?

Table of Contents

Isn't it crazy that...

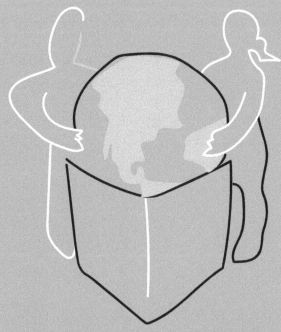

people expect us to think outside the box when we've helped to construct it?

Preface

This is a book of questions (?) interspersed with short chapters. (One very short chapter.)

The over-arching question is:

Isn't it kind of funny that we don't live in paradise?

Many readers will react, with all the reasons why things, bad as they are, pretty much have to stay that way. Because "that's the way things are."

But they don't have to stay that way, and they won't.

Because the earth is evolving, consciousness is evolving, and it's going on in millions of people all over the planet. It's unstoppable. That's the beauty of it. Because no matter how bleak or dire the situation may seem to be, consciousness is moving forward, in and through us.

We are part of that movement. Once we realize our true identity, we see our intimate connection to all life on the planet, and especially to each other. That's a glimpse of heaven.

There's no need to wait for the afterlife for fulfillment. The dimension of spaciousness (the kingdom of heaven) is within each of us.

Right now, at this moment.

Many of the questions simply point out the discrepancy between what we are and what we could be. For example, it's ludicrous that animals and plants are better stewards of the earth than we are. Or that trees and animals take better care of each other than we do.

Some of the questions might even cause you to momentarily stop your usual thought patterns. If that should happen, pay attention to the break or gap created. By becoming aware of the gap in our stream of thoughts, there's an opportunity for space to enter.

Space

Chapter 1

The most important part of a room is space. Empty space

No space: no room to move, to maneuver. You can't even enter a room filled with furniture, boxes of papers and useless junk.

There is a similarity on the non-physical level. If our minds are churning out thoughts, constantly thinking while we're awake—as is true for most human beings—then there's no room for anything to enter.

That wouldn't be a problem except that it means we are **unconscious.**

If we're not aware that we're thinking, we're living in a sort of dream state. You could say that "we're being thought" rather than that "we're thinking." Because thinking has taken us over. Captured us. How do we know that's true? Because we are not even aware of it (that we're thinking).

Once you see that, you can awaken from the dream state, observe the fact that you're thinking, having thoughts. In that instance you have created a *gap,* a second or a few seconds in which there's *no-thought.*

That's a Mini-Big-Bang on the way to your creation or re-creation. Because at your birth you were already a Big-Bang-Baby, a bright star in the constellation, smiling joyfully at your beautiful surroundings, whatever they may have been.

Look into the eyes of a baby. Your recognition will light up his/her eyes, and you will see in them a reflection of yourself.

That's the beginning of opening up the closed, packed closet of our minds, and allowing the vast spaciousness of the universe to enter (not all at once, mind you!) and revitalize our lives.

Because our true identity is consciousness. We're not born to be happy, but to become conscious (which of course includes joy).

We are spacious, even on the physical level. Every atom is mostly space, and there's 100 trillion atoms in every cell of the body.

By opening up our inner space we are inviting consciousness.

And we then see that there's no space between ourselves, between you and me.

Mine the gap!

Isn't it weird that...

as babies we
are perfect,
and by
adulthood we
are trashed,
paying dear
money to learn
what we
forgot/left
behind?

Isn't it weird that...

as babies we
are perfect,
and by
adulthood we
are trashed,
paying dear
money to learn
what we
forgot/left
behind?

Cars´R us Part 1

Chapter 2

Cars are a part of us.

What would a "carless world" look like?

Armageddon! Millions of jobs lost!

Billions of asphalt roads going to weeds!

Trillions of dollars would have to be spent elsewhere.

Cities designed around cars would have identity crises.

How will parking lots feel? Empty! Sad.

Freeways: what would become of them? Lonely. Useless. Decrepit.

Mom and pop fossil fuel stores would face bankruptcy!

What about insurance? Billboards? Road rage? Ambulances, toll trucks, hitchhikers, deer signs?

What would we put in our garage? (Silly question)

It's not easy to imagine a car-less world. That says something right there. And the people who poo-poo this notion would easily demolish it: the status quo is threatened.

Isn't it hard to believe...

that we still have cars?

"Life would come to a screeching halt without cars," they would say. Fear mongers dispatched everywhere to dispel any such notion.

But entertain it anyway. Imagine it, just empty your car-riddled mind with its grid-like rational structure, and envision how incredibly beautiful, and quiet, and serene a world without cars would be.

We could still travel. Instead of crowded trains and subways, we could have our trains and buses designed by children. They will be fun places to be, so that the journey is as important and interesting as the destination.

Remember how fun and adventurous the first cars were? Open to the outside world and to people?

Now even the windows don't look out. Time to stop. It's over.

Thinking

Chapter 3

As Shakespeare observed,

"Nothing is evil in the world lest thinking make it so."

Thinking can be very useful if used for what it's intended: finding practical solutions to problems, and/or creating. Used to make bigger and better bombs, it's not useful.

And if we spend all of our waking hours lost in thought, It's not a good use of our time.

It's estimated that we think 12,000 to 18,000 thoughts a day. **80% of them are negative. 95% are the same as yesterday's.**

Recycled thoughts do not help the environment!

Ever notice the repetitive cycle of your thoughts?

Thinking is also entwined with our ego. When we're thinking, we're usually judging other people, in the service of our ego, to inflate it.

Isn't it curious that...

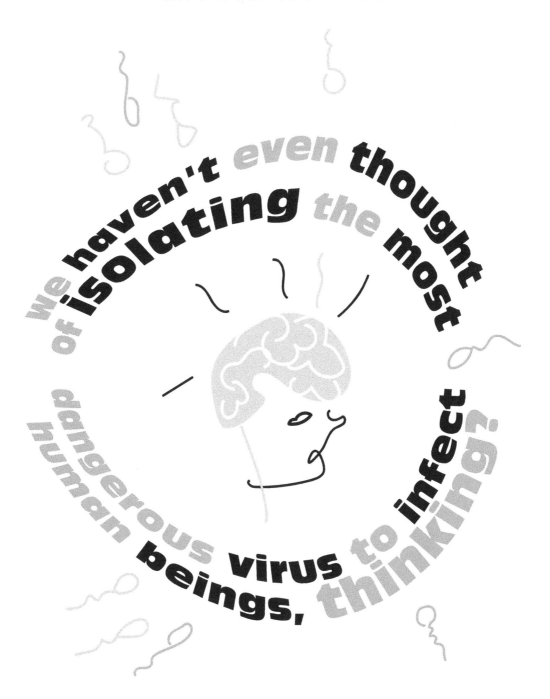

we haven't even thought of isolating the most dangerous virus to infect human beings, thinking?

But we cannot not-think. It's not even useful to try. Stop thinking about the elephant in the room! You can't.

But you can become aware that you're thinking about the elephant in the room. Then you can put your attention elsewhere, thereby leaving the elephant in a cul-de-sac.

Once you're aware of the fact that you're thinking, you create a gap, and in that brief interval, you're not thinking.

That's a milestone!

Mind the gap.

If thoughts can cause the growth of plants, wouldn't that work with human beings even better?

Time

Chapter 4

**Time doesn't exist.
There's no past,
no future.**

It's about time!

But it's never about time.

It's about something else.

It's about thinking.

Time doesn't exist. There's no past, no future. Only the present moment right now as you're reading this sentence.

The animal kingdom knows no time. Humans, before time came to be "kept," relied on nature's cycles and rhythms. As we "think our way through the day," looking at our watches, keeping track of time, are we keeping time or is it keeping us?

Try going for a day (when you have no appointments to make) without knowing what time it is. You might be amazed. We have an inner clock. We can tell ourselves "I want to wake up at 6 AM tomorrow morning." And it can work (might need some fine tuning).

Time is mostly about thinking. I'm constantly thinking about what I have to do and how much time I have left.

Time stands still (no measuring it or awareness of it) when we're not thinking, when we're totally engaged: dancing, surfing, rock climbing, skydiving.

People engage in extreme sports to capture the "high" of not thinking.

The gap doesn't mind.

Isn't it kind of funny that...

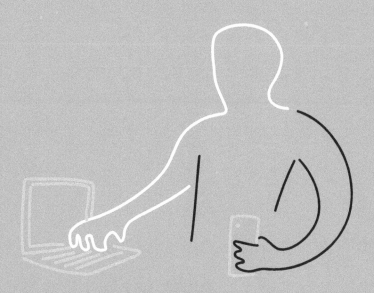

we're too
busy to
spend time
with the
most
important of our
part our
self inner being?

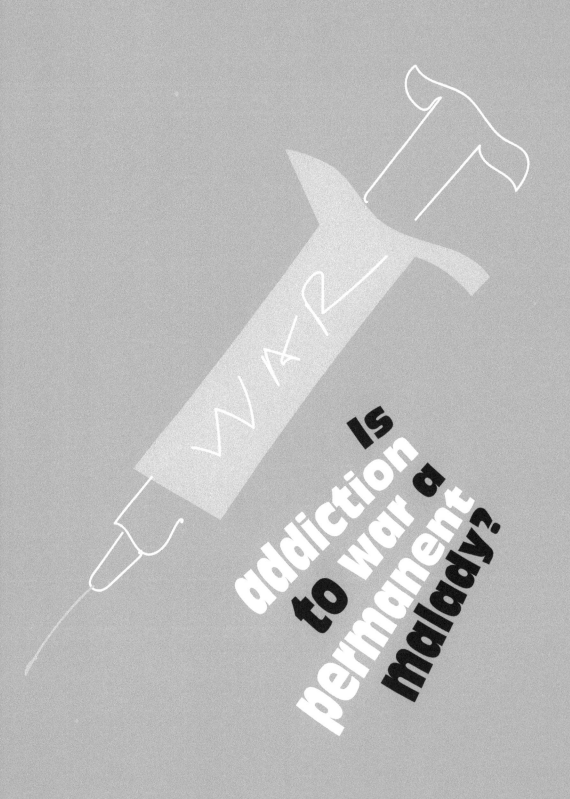

War

Chapter 5

War: No More.
War is boring.

The objective of war is to destroy. The exact opposite of what human nature, according to its original factory settings, is designed to do.

Edict of the people: no guns, bombs, or bullets will be allowed to leave one country's borders for another. BB guns? Maybe, but countries can make their own BB guns. Squirt guns, OK.

The very few people of the even fewer nations that believe in war and attempt to enlist other nations in this deadly mind-narcotic will be themselves enlisted in a 12-step program: People Addicted to War.

13th step: to spend a year in each country that has unexploded ordinance buried underground. And dig every day.

The proper response to war: Really? Trying to be funny? We've only been doing that since the dawn of civilization.

War, new definition: a former activity engaged in by human beings who had been deprived of their senses.

War-like: someone who resembles conflict, fighting himself in his mind; someone at war with himself.

Wargames: activity of grown adults, not yet mature

Isn't it almost hilarious that...

BOOMM?

people still be-
lieve that a
war's
solution?

Isn't it crazy that...

Cars´R us _{Part 2}

Chapter 6

Cars: motorized devices that go around with an invisible straw sucking juice out of the earth, another straw shooting gases into the outside air.

We don't have cars. They have us.
They demand to be fed expensive food. Demand insurance in case they need to go to the body shop for some cosmetic repairs. Demand space to be parked. Demand to be driven. Demand that we be emotionally involved while driving them.

And in return they emit gases, dangerous chemical-laden air everywhere we take them. And the nice tires they require spin off tiny particles that can kill marine life, like dolphins in the San Francisco Bay.

And we breathe in the microscopic rubber particles. Tire manufacturers insist that tire dust helps our mind-gears go faster.

They require us to spend hours inside of them every day, and we're expected to compete or jostle for position with others of their kind on city streets and highways, and even get emotionally involved on their behalf, even if it means endangering ourselves.

They don't really care about us going to the hospital, they know they'll come out looking even better when we take them in for plastic surgery. And they won't feel a thing.

They have us right where they want us: addicted. We can't give them up, they're part of us, part of our fabric, of our family. Sometimes we even name them, polish their skin lovingly and even talk to them.

Isn't it kind of strange that...

some parents spend more time in their cars than with their kids?

Consciousness

Chapter 7

> Consciousness is like a tiny seed buried deep within each of us. In many humans, the seed never finds the light of day, never receives the rain of recognition to bring it to life

But it's never too late. Like now.

Once you become aware that you're thinking, you're already becoming more conscious. You can now observe your thoughts. You are entering the doorway into your inner self, the true self that has been covered over, buried under all the recycled trash of the thinking mind.

The thinking mind would rather you don't discover and nurture the seed of self-awareness. Because the stronger your consciousness becomes, the less control the thinking mind will exert over you.

When you are no longer dominated by thinking, you're no longer in the grip of the ego.

But the ego will not go quietly.

It mightily minds any gaps

Isn't it mind-boggling that...

we are able
to relate
more warmly
to animals
than to
human
beings?

Death

Chapter 8

We don't do death. The END.

Because we think the ending is the end. Instead of the beginning.

Look at the floor of a forest where death forges an explosion of new life.

Our way of life necessitates the exclusion of death. We're not allowed to see it. We are protected from it. It doesn't fit into the framework of our life, which is concentrated on "doing" rather than "being."

Death is sacred. It's a beautiful, precious time. If we can allow it, accept it.

It's a holy moment when we transition from the physical form/body we've inhabited for a brief period, to form-less consciousness.

Isn't it funny that...

the next most important thing in life, death, is absent in our lives?

It's the same consciousness that we have now. We can know that, experience that now, and then death takes on a different meaning. We no longer need to fear it. We can embrace it. At the same time, we can relish even more the time we have left.

Death frees us to experience the joy of life.

We need to make death's acquaintance, introduce ourselves and get comfortable being in the same room with the hooded figure of death. He'll be coming for us. But we can beat him to it!

Ideally, we die before we actually die. Before the physical body dies, we can let our mind-dominated ego die. That's the part of us that keeps us bogged down in the "poor me, why is life so hard and I have so many problems" script.

It's the suffering melodrama, the typical movie story, and it makes up the daily news cycle.

When we let that part go, life truly begins. And everything starts to connect, just like the forest floor that looks mangled and chaotic, but is in perfect order, everything intimately connected.

Isn't it weird that...

we don't really expect people to die?

10 FEET

Isn't it astounding that...

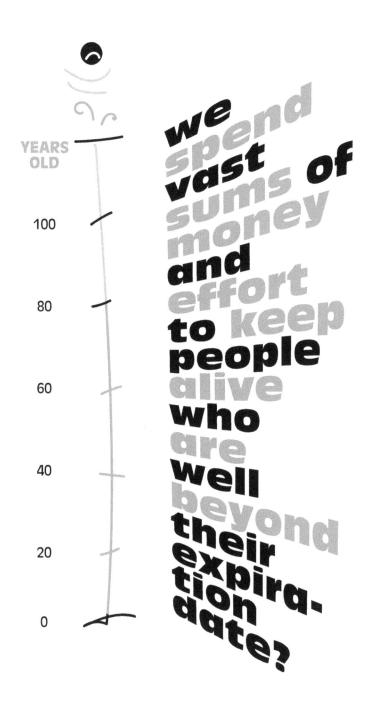

YEARS OLD

100

80

60

40

20

0

we spend vast sums of money and effort to keep people alive who are well beyond their expira- tion date?

Food

Chapter 9

Food connects us to the earth which is a conscious organism.

The food we eat to feed the physical body also plays a part in nourishing our non-physical self, or spiritual side.

Food connects us to the earth which is a conscious organism.

The more conscious we become, the closer we want to connect to the source that nourishes us, mother earth.

Whether you grow your own vegetables, get them from the co-op, or a local farmers market, your participation ensures health benefits for your body and your mind/spirit. Which includes your connection to the human beings who grew the food and brought it to you.

Getting your fruits and vegetables fresh will ensure that you get the maximum nutrients possible, something not possible with packaged and processed foods.

The body is a single organism. We cannot pretend that there's no cost involved in eating unhealthy foods. At some point we will pay the price in full, physically and mentally.

The body prefers to be treated according to the "factory settings."

It has a junk detector. The body lets us know when we are not treating it right.

And it doesn't lie.

But the mind does.

Mind the Pap

Isn't it kind of crazy that...

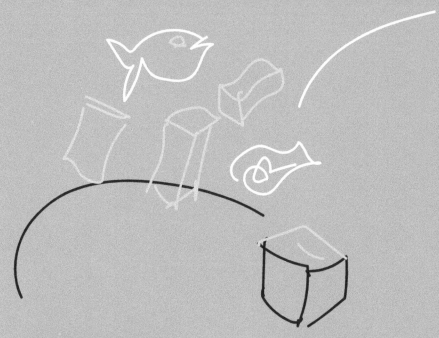

most of the food we eat lacks the essential nutrients we need?

Isn't it bizarre that being...

Human Beings

Chapter 10

Human beings are the most underrated species on planet earth.

This according to *Poor Standards*, the species-rating firm that decides on the best species to invest in. Humans have one of the lowest scores, usually rated as "high risk" and often included with junk bonds and/or hedge funds.

All of the other species, especially the elephants and dolphins, have long recognized this and have played along with humans and their little charades, hoping they would come to their senses.

Human beings, having more ability to express the "joy of being" than their cousins, nonetheless have been slow to take advantage of this. In fact, "joy" is not listed as one of their attributes.

Trees have recently revealed their vast underground web of interconnectedness, hoping that humans could learn how it works.

Isn't it kind of funny that...

trees are smarter than human beings?

Isn't it ironic that...

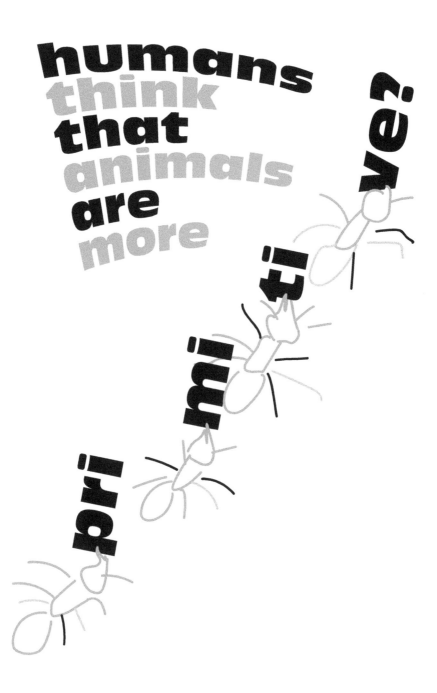

humans think that animals are more primitive?

All of the animal species have demonstrated simple patterns of cooperation and care for each other, but humans insist that these don't apply to them. They claim to be exceptional.

When in fact, human beings could benefit immensely by simply trying to imitate their "more primitive" cousin species.

However, humans' standing has been rising in the late 20th and early 21st-century. There are a significant number of human beings who recognize their kinship with the natural world: trees, flowers, dogs, cats and even the sky and stars.

They are beginning to recognize the joy of being human.

These humans recognize their kinship with each other, like the vast root system of trees. They see their intricate connection with each other, something the animal kingdom has always "known."

Human beings are finally coming into their own. Their rightful place in the universe. Seeing themselves in each other as well as in the rest of nature.

Some human beings see a new earth emerging.

Maybe it's time to make an investment.

Isn't it kind of silly that...

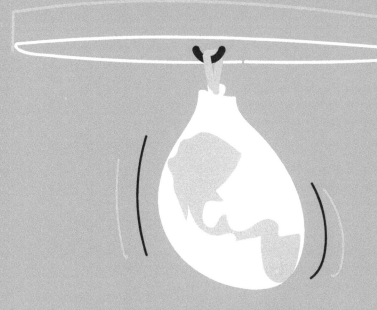

many
humans
argue
or
fight
with
reality,
refusing
to
accept
what
is?

Being and Doing

Chapter 11

> We know how *to do.*
> How *to be?* Not so much.

You got out of bed this morning. First thought/question: what will I do today? And away we go. We know how *to do.* How *to be?* Not so much.

It's instilled in us from early on. We are programmed *to do,* to *keep busy, don't stop.*

But if we don't find a balance between being and doing, we will pay. If our life is all about doing, doing, doing—non-stop—we'll be stressing our delicate system out of balance.

When a gauge on our car blinks, indicating something needs to be looked at, we can simply ignore it—after all the car's humming along fine—but down the road it might just stop altogether. Our bodies are somewhat similar.

If we don't pay attention to the cues and signals that our body is sending out, the signals may get stronger until our hand is forced.

Keep in mind: **Life works.** It works for flowers and trees, cats and dogs, life in general—so why shouldn't it work for human beings? Animals are in a "being state," no thought. We can learn about "being" from cats and dogs. Nature is also an avenue into "being."

Eckhart Tolle, renowned spiritual teacher, calls dogs the *Guardians of Being.* When our pet dies, we probably miss their being-ness, what we see when we look into their eyes, more than their physical body.

Ideally, "being" and "doing" can coalesce in the same activity. If we are aware while we're doing, whatever the activity might be: brushing our teeth, opening a door or window, turning the key in the lock, or breathing, we can be in a being/doing state at the same time.

Whether it's at work, or driving or cooking—if we are not thinking—we are in a "being" state.

Alternatively, if I'm trying to meditate, I'm in a "doing" state, not a "being" state. I'm making an effort and probably thinking about it, causing stress.

To introduce more "being" into our doing-filled life, we need to get back to our true identity, nourish the seed of awareness that we're uncovering inside ourselves. By becoming more aware of our daily activities, we can begin a re-orientation process, which, once set in motion, can gradually bring ourselves, bit by bit, back to a more balanced state.

We don't need to go to an ashram. We don't need more time. We don't need to wait.

Keep in mind that "getting there" is not the goal. At any moment of the day, when we're aware of what we're doing, or aware of the fact that we're conscious—we are there. We are not looking toward the future.

The process of moving towards balance, of becoming more conscious, is not difficult. It can be a natural process. Our bodies, our physical/psychic organisms, naturally want (us) to be in a healthy, joyful state. We just need to get out of the way, allow and accept (not resist) what life puts on our plate. It's that simple.

Enjoy the smorgasbord of life. It can be quite delicious. And the flavors are always changing.

Awareness

Chapter 12

Human beings have one enormous advantage over the rest of the living organisms on the planet Earth. Awareness.

We can sense the fact that we are now reading these words. That's our experience at this moment. But now, we are *attending to the fact that we are reading the words*.

That involves a bit of a jump: not just reading the words, but realizing, being aware, that we are reading the words.

That's a huge difference! We could probably teach chimps to read a few words or to speak a few words, but they would most likely not *be aware* of the experience of doing so.

We can be aware of our breathing, that we are now breathing. In and out. We can feel the breath entering and leaving our mouth, even see our bellies rising and falling or expanding and contracting. It's a sensual experience. We can see it and feel it.

But rather than being aware of our breathing, or of reading some words, or driving, etc., we are usually preoccupied with our thoughts. Thinking our way through life *indirectly,* rather than experiencing it *directly.*

Isn't it incredible that...

most humans don't know that they are thinking?

Isn't it kind of foolish that...

many humans
spend their
whole lifetime
waiting for
their life to
start?

In other words, we don't use our tremendous advantage, the most distinguishing part of our repertoire as a human being.

Does it matter? It does if we want to actually be a human being instead of a vegetable!

Because when we are not aware of what we're doing, we've dropped below the threshold of "being human." We're simply existing in a dream-like state, subject to whatever whims and fancies come our way in the form of opinions and stories from outside ourselves. Which can be very confusing. And disorienting. Exhibit A: the *Daily News*.

Practice noticing—what you're doing, whatever is in your immediate surroundings and/or experience. When we notice, focus our attention on the pen we're using, or the water coming out of the faucet, the toothbrush we're using—the smallest, seemingly unimportant details of our life—we are aware that we are engaged in that action.

After a few baby steps, we can practice being aware while in the presence of other human beings. That's a big challenge which can bring huge dividends.

Awareness enriches our human experience. It makes growth possible.

If we're not aware of what we do today, tomorrow will probably be a repeat.

Not that different from a tree. In fact, notice the tree. We can learn something from it, from its stillness.

Energy

Chapter 13

Human beings need energy. We get survival energy from the food, water, and air that we take in.

To thrive, humans need psychic energy, energy derived from other humans, usually in exchange. Of course, depending on the degree of consciousness, the exchange may be lopsided. A depressed person might suck the energy from a happy friend, leaving the friend depleted.

Fully conscious humans realize their connection to Energy Itself. They sense it within themselves, and they are impelled to express it.

We transmit our energy to others, whether negative or positive. There can be a room full of happy people at a party, and someone enters the room in a state of anger.

Isn't it surprising that...

We believe that our physical bodies are the most real part of ourselves?

Isn't it funny that...

we do not
take seriously
someone who is
smiling or
laughing?

The "room" instantly reacts, the balloon of happy feelings is punctured, the room deflates.

The opposite occurs as well. Sometimes the party seems to be dragging along as if pulling a heavy weight. An energized, joyful person arrives and the atmosphere changes. People perk up, as if woken from slumber.

Energy is like a virus transmitted from person to person.

Laughter, also a form of energy exchange, is contagious. If someone, even a stranger, near me starts to laugh, my facial features automatically start to relax, at first into a smile, and maybe even a laugh.

Cars´R Us Part 3

Chapter 14

**Cars cost a lot!
Average yearly cost:
$5000 to $20,000.**

Average number of headaches: many.

Number of pills to bring down the
stress level: anybody's guess!

Don't forget: Insurance costs, medical
costs, time waiting for a tow truck,
stress levels, road rage, fossil fuels,
pollution, time spent at stop lights,
fumes and fuming!

Still, it was a nice experiment. Didn't
quite work out to our advantage.
Out with them!

Just imagine! All the new natural
habitat restored, the new car-less
neighborhood. A downtown with no
cars. Tables set up for eating on car-less
streets. Kids playing in the street.

Our life.

Isn't it strange that...

city planners'
first priority is
traffic/cars
and streets
instead of
children?

People could still keep their cars if they want, but the cost of owning a car would simply go up gradually as the various expenses are gradually added in, eventually making it very difficult to own one.

For example, the cost of gasoline would include the impact of extraction, the infrastructure needed to get it from the ground to the hose that's dispensing it into your car, the cost of the little screens selling you ads while you pump gas.

It would include the destruction of habitat involved in drilling for oil, the toxic chemicals left on the ground that would need to be cleaned up and disposed of, the chemicals released into the air from the combustion of the gasoline.

The construction of new highways and bridges, maintenance of entryways and culverts. The erasure of graffiti found on freeway signs.

How high would the price of gasoline go, $15 a gallon? $50?

The true cost of owning a car would rise dramatically. When you take out all of the subsidies that the government pays for, oops, I mean that we pay for, it's a different story altogether.

Eventually, it might take a few years, the few that can afford a car would look so silly and out of place—it would be just the opposite of status—people would laugh at them and pretty soon they would abandon them, simply walk away from them.

We could still visit them, in a museum.

Isn't it amazing that...

we think of ourselves as "merely human" when we're actually part of Being Itself, each of us a tiny replica of the universe?

And now a word from our sponsor...

Chapter 15

This is It: Finding Out

Chapter 16

Who we are!
Who are we?

Close your eyes, sit up in a comfortable chair, take a few deep breaths to start, then get into a regular breathing pattern while you observe a big blue sky in your mind. If thoughts arise, and they will, let them float by as clouds across the horizon of your blue, spacious sky-mind. Above all, don't fight them: simply noticing them is already ample attention.

You are not trying to see or to visualize anything.

You are simply being open and receptive, allowing and inviting quiet and stillness into your body and mind, becoming totally relaxed in the process.

That's it. You did it! You had a few seconds of non-thinking.

In this simple exercise, which quiets (somewhat) the thinking mind, we are making contact with the "seed" within. Opening a route into our inner self, our true self.

The experience of having no thoughts in our head can be unnerving because it's so unusual. But it's not exactly a vacuum.

When we're not thinking, but still conscious, we're inviting/allowing ourselves to be in contact with the Intelligence of the Universe. With Consciousness.

It's a start. And our ego-thinking-mind will say: "This is stupid. Didn't work, did it? I knew it wouldn't. I'd ask for my money back! This book is trash!"

There is a conspiracy at work within each of us. It's our ego conspiring to keep us locked into the nightmarish dream called reality. "Because" it says, "that's where the action is!"

And we will keep listening to it, till we're ready to stop.

Mind the crap.

Isn't it mind-blowing that...

we never really find out who we are, or why we're here?

Isn't it kind of silly that...

adults don't
realize how
much they
can learn
from little
kids?

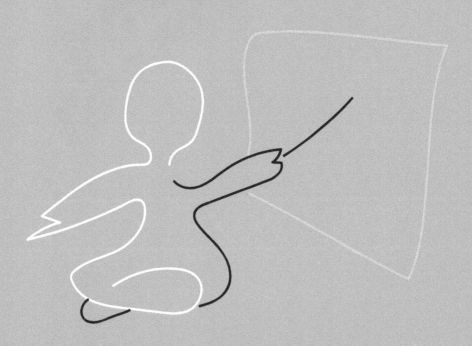

Kids 'R Us

Chapter 17

Kids can be our best teachers. If we are willing to learn.

Babies are absolutely astounding creatures! If we give them what they need, they will dazzle us with their stunning beauty and perfection.

They can pull us into their sacred world and help us to remember.

For the first few years, they are still in-between: residing in the magical world of one-ness while taking baby steps into the very different world that we live in, referred to as reality.

They are not yet preoccupied with/ by thinking. They're experiencing the world through their body and their senses rather than through their mind.

Their world is one of magical realism, a let's-pretend world. They are conscious, living from moment to moment.

They can teach us to play again! They're happy to show us how.

As we move into the New Earth, parents and children will be able to spend as much time together as they desire, thereby minimizing, if not eliminating altogether, problems down the road.

In the meantime, we can make the time less mean by accepting their lessons.

we
don't
teach
kids in
kindergarten
that thoughts are
not real?

Isn't it sad that...

adults are the
most gloomy,
depressed
species on
earth?

Toolkit

Chapter 18

Obviously, you will need a few things if you're to transform your life, basically from hell to heaven (hand basket not required).

Like an assortment of books, tapes, podcasts and Lectures 'R Us.

A few mountain retreats in the Himalayas or fasting in your backyard for 40 days (nights optional).

Not to mention: 400 hours listening to Masters and Mistresses on Tape: Finding Life's Inner Secret Passageways to Your Inner Treasures and Wallet.

Not.

You don't need one thing in addition to what you already have.

Yourself.

You are already perfect. Just as when you were born. You only need to realize/ see that.

You have within yourself all you will ever need to become the magnificent creature you naturally are, a conscious human being.

You are indeed priceless!

Isn't it mind-boggling that...

we actually measure our worth in dollars as in "he's got to be worth 5 million?"

Isn't it amazing that...

we don't realize that

each person's identity conceals a vast treasure waiting to be opened up?

Evolution

Chapter 19

We are nearing the end of the thinking-dominated period of history, lasting from the beginning of thought till today.

Thinking will not end, but will be put to creative and peaceful ends, rather than destructive and war-like ends.

Thousands, more likely millions, of people all over the world are now on the journey toward the New Earth. The journey is within. It begins as an individual pilgrimage. When we find our bearings, we move out, spreading our wings.

Now that we're aware of the suffering that excessive thinking causes, not just to ourselves, but to those around us as well, there's no going back. We can never return, nor would we want to.

Once you get a glimpse of Shangri-La, you're hooked (in a good way).

There's still suffering to endure, because without it, we won't move from our comfortable status quo. We suffer untill we no longer need to suffer.

Evolution is relentless. The universe wants to be conscious. We are an expression of that. And our bodies, our very selves, want to be healthy and they will drive us constantly to become healthy, to be more and more conscious.

Nothing can be more beautiful than that!

Mind that.

Isn't it kind of screwy that...

we allow ourselves
to be put in
opposition to our
neighbors, friends
and even family, just
on the basis of a few
words or a belief?

The New Earth

Chapter 20

The world we see around us: the cities made up of factories, housing developments, palatial mansions, shantytowns near the dump, asphalt roads, sidewalks, parks, all of it—didn't just happen by accident.

It's 100% our creation. All of it, the beautiful and the ugly, the healthy and the toxic elements—it's ours!

Yes, we are born into it, but we continue it. Continue to support it and uphold it.

But no longer. We now know that when we are aligned with our true nature and with the universe, we can do anything.

It's time to re-imagine it. Just as we are re-imagining ourselves, as we find our identity, we can imagine what the New Earth will look like. And bring it into existence. No need to wait for judgment day. We can have our New Earth/Heaven now.

The current model that we inhabit was formed from a framework of competition and greed. The new model will evolve from a mind graced with harmony and creativity.

Isn't it ironic that...

human beings, the most advanced species by far, are the most destructive species on earth?

Now that we are putting thought into its rightful place, in the "backseat" so to speak, the need for suffering greatly diminishes.

There's no need to wait any longer. Once we awaken to our true identity and recognize our shared consciousness with nature and with each other, we are already into a new realm of our "own" (it's not really ours) creation, one that is in alignment with the universe, of which we are an important part.

The world we are creating will be informed by our deep sense of connection: with nature, each other and the Universe. It will be a world infused with joy. One full of creativity: play, dance, music and the other arts.

It will look more like child's play. Each day different. Each day a fresh creation.

Wow! I can't wait.

We don't have to!

It's in the gap.

It's now.

Afterword

Take a deep breath. Now take another one, this time without thinking. So that you can be conscious of the fact that you're breathing.

By becoming aware of what we're doing for just a few minutes every day, or taking a few conscious breaths during the day, we can become a different human being. And achieve a level of joy and satisfaction we didn't think possible. Awareness is key: we cannot be aware when we're lost in thought.

Some of the questions in this book challenge how we see things. A few chapters might jar your assumptions or beliefs.

Reality is neither good nor bad. It simply is. We can snarl at it and fight it, or laugh at it and accept it.

The overall purpose of this book is to playfully jog your mind and hopefully bring a smile. The illustrations are beautifully designed to do just that.

After all, we are here to savor the beauty and joy of life. When we are aware, we are able to appreciate the incredible majesty in a drop of water. **That changes everything.**

About the Author Jerry Schaefer

I grew up in Cut Bank, Montana, a small town influenced by the nearby Blackfoot Indian Reservation. My best friend at Saint Margaret's Grade School was a Blackfoot Indian, "Beaver" Bird.

I've always been looking for answers, trying to make sense of life. At 16, when Brad, a popular, good-looking kid in Cut Bank, married a girl that I thought was "ugly," it threw my worldview into smithereens. How is this possible?

The questions continued into the monastery, college, the army, graduate school, two marriages. At 68, I found the answer in *The Power of Now*, by Eckhart Tolle—THINKING. That's what I'd been doing my whole life, creating enormous suffering for myself.

As I dug myself out of the pit of self-pity, I naturally wanted to express the joy I felt.

I've always enjoyed playing with words. The subjects that I write about these days are influenced by the changed version of reality that I now inhabit.

How is it changed? I am now able to actually talk to a person and listen to what they're saying, instead of thinking about what I'm going to say back to them. Or worse, judging them by their words or how they look. What a difference!

Previous books include: *Guide to Swifter and Deeper Thoughts* (1987, unavailable); *Women: Down through the Ages, How Lies Have Shaped Our Lives* (2007); *The Story of You* (Shires Press, 2019); *Cruising through the Teens, Easier Than It Seems* (Shires Press, 2021).

I have two websites: *expandjoy.com* and *cruisingtheteenseasierthanitseems.com*, and a third blog site, *expandingjoys.com*.

The Illustrator Gabriel Berrón

Born and raised in Mexico City, as a child I filled my notebooks with all sorts of drawings in the margins.

I studied graphic design in Mexico, then I completed a masters degree at the Academy of Fine Arts in Warsaw, Poland.

After working a few years as an art director for different agencies, I started my own more than 20 years ago. Since then we have developed a myriad of projects for different national and international companies, solving a variety of graphic needs.

I am passionate about envisioning concepts through the media of illustrations, painting, photography, as well as design in all its branches.

I appreciate the opportunity to work with this great team again, and I am proud to show this book as part of my portfolio.

The Designer Anne Pace

With a degree from the School of Visual Arts in NYC, I began working as a freelance illustrator. Realizing that I needed to "work" for a living, I learned graphic design from the bottom up, working as a layout artist in the days before computers.

Through the years I've worn many hats in the marketing and publishing industries. Currently I am a freelance graphic designer, among other things.

I make my home in Vermont, near one of the last working dairy farms, with my border collie Rhynn. I find peace here.

Working with these two talented individuals to convey Jerry's message has been a great privilege.

CPSIA information can be obtained
at www.ICGtesting.com
Printed in the USA
JSHW052303071221
21044JS00003B/10

Made in the USA
San Bernardino, CA
27 September 2014